D0553573

HOWE

Really Big Cats

By Allan Fowler

Consultants

Linda Cornwell, Learning Resource Consultant,
Indiana Department of Education

Sharyn Fenwick, Elementary Science/Math Specialist,
Gustavus Adolphus College, St. Peter, Minnesota

Children's Press®
A Division of Grolier Publishing
New York   London   Hong Kong   Sydney
Danbury, Connecticut

Visit Children's Press® on the Internet at:
http://publishing.grolier.com

Designer: Herman Adler Design Group

Library of Congress Cataloging-in-Publication Data

Fowler, Allan.
    Really big cats / by Allan Fowler.
      p. cm. — (Rookie read-about science)
    Includes index.
    Summary: An introduction to the habits and habitats of lions, tigers, leopards, and jaguars.
    ISBN 0-516-20805-5 (lib. bdg.)   0-516-26367-6 (pbk.)
    1. Panthera—Juvenile literature. [1. Panthera. 2. Cats.] I. Title. II. Series.
QL737.C23F685   1998   97-17895
599.755—dc21   CIP
                                            AC

Cats may make fine pets.
They are small and cuddly,
gentle and quiet. Of course
we are talking about house
cats. There are other
members of the cat family
that you
could not
keep as
pets . . .

. . . the big cats. Biggest of all are lions and tigers. Male lions and tigers can weigh up to 500 pounds (227 kilograms). That's as much as two or three grown-ups!

The females usually weigh
a little less. Only the male
lions have manes, those
collars of long, heavy hair
around their heads.

Most lions live in Africa.
Many years ago, they could
be found in Europe and Asia.
Today, no lions live there,
except for a few in India.

Young lions, their parents, aunts, and cousins live in groups called prides. There are up to about 30 lions in a pride.

Female lions, or lionesses, do most of the hunting. They hunt only when the pride is hungry.

Male lions guard the pride's territory.

Lions eat animals, such as zebras and antelopes. They do not often attack people if they are left alone.

Another big cat, the Bengal tiger, lives in warm southern parts of Asia.

Siberian tigers live in the colder north. There are no tigers in Africa.

Most tigers' fur is brownish-
orange between their stripes
and white on their throats,
bellies, and the inner parts
of their legs.

A few tigers are white between their stripes. Tigers don't live in groups the way lions do. They hunt alone, usually at night. They are nocturnal.

Leopards are another type of big cat. They live in Asia and Africa. Most leopards have light tan coats with black spots. A cluster of spots is called a rosette.

Snow leopards have whitish fur with spots. They live in the cold mountain regions of Asia.

A leopard may give birth to
a litter of three or four cubs,
some black and some spotted.

Black leopards are often called panthers.

Leopards can run fast,
climb trees easily, and
leap far.

They hunt birds, reptiles,
and mammals, usually
at night.

The largest leopards are
about half the size of
tigers or lions.

19

Jaguars look a lot like leopards. Here's how to tell them apart. A jaguar has spots in the center of its rosettes.

A leopard does not.

Jaguars are also a little
heavier than leopards.

Jaguars live in forests and grasslands in Central and South America.

24

Hunters have reduced the numbers of lions, tigers, leopards, and jaguars.

People have moved into lands where these beautiful animals once roamed free.

There is still hope that big cats will not vanish.

Today, in African game reserves, lions are protected.

They may only be "hunted" with cameras.

Zoos and game parks around the world are making sure that lots of cubs are born and are raised to be healthy adults.

Cubs are born in litters of
two to four. The cubs are
cute and playful. They
would make fine pets—if
only they didn't grow so fast.

After all, who wants a 500-pound cat around the house?

Words You Know

game reserve

lion

lioness

jaguar

leopard

panther

tiger

mane

rosettes

cubs

litter

pride

31

Index

About the Author

Allan Fowler is a freelance writer with a background in advertising. Born in New York, he now lives in Chicago and enjoys traveling.

Photo Credits

©: Alan & Sandy Carey: 5, 10, 16, 22, 28, 29, 30 bottom left, 31 bottom center, 31 center, 31 bottom left; Ellis Nature Photography: 24 (Gerry Ellis), 15 (Terry Whitaker), 4, 11, 13, 31 middle left (Konrad Wothe); Photo Researchers: 14, 3 (Mark Burnett), cover (Alan D. Carey), 21 (Tim Davis), 23, 31 top left (Tom & Pat Leeson), 17, 20, 27, 30 top, 31 top right, 31 middle right (Renee Lynn); Visuals Unlimited: 12 (Milton H. Tierney Jr.), 6 (Leonard Lee Rue III), 8, 19, 30 bottom right, 31 top center (Joe McDonald), 7, 31 bottom right (Will Troyer).